Greenhouse Gardening for Beginners

Ultimate Guide to Growing Organic Vegetables and Fruits. How to Build Your Own Greenhouse and Grow Amazing Year-Round Organic Vegetables, Fruits, Herbs and Flowers

© Copyright by **Kevin S. Stevenson**

Kevin S. Stevenson
Greenhouse Gardening For Beginners

© Copyright 2023 by Kevin S. Stevenson - **All rights reserved.**

This Book is provided with the sole purpose of providing relevant information on a specific topic for which every reasonable effort has been made to ensure that it is both accurate and reasonable. Nevertheless, by purchasing this Book, you consent to the fact that the author, as well as the publisher, are in no way experts on the topics contained herein, regardless of any claims as such that may be made within. As such, any suggestions or recommendations that are made within are done so purely for entertainment value. It is recommended that you always consult a professional prior to undertaking any of the advice or techniques discussed within.

This is a legally binding declaration that is considered both valid and fair by both the Committee of Publishers Association and the American Bar Association and should be considered as legally binding within the United States.

The reproduction, transmission, and duplication of any of the content found herein, including any specific or extended information, will be done as an illegal act regardless of the end form the information ultimately takes. This includes copied versions of the work, both physical, digital, and audio, unless express consent of the Publisher is provided beforehand. Any additional rights reserved.

Furthermore, the information that can be found within the pages described forthwith shall be considered both accurate and truthful when it comes to the recounting of facts. As such, any use, correct or incorrect, of the provided information will render the Publisher free of responsibility as to the actions taken outside of their direct purview. Regardless, there are zero scenarios where the original author or the Publisher can be deemed liable in any fashion for any damages or hardships that may result from any of the information discussed herein.

Additionally, the information in the following pages is intended only for informational purposes and should thus be thought of as universal. As befitting its nature, it is presented without assurance regarding its prolonged validity or interim quality. Trademarks that are mentioned are done without written consent and can in no way be considered an endorsement from the trademark holder.

Kevin S. Stevenson
Greenhouse Gardening For Beginners

Table of Contents

INTRODUCTION 7
CHAPTER 1 - Types of Greenhouses 11
   Types of greenhouses 13
      Agrotextiles 16
      Hydroponic greenhouses 17
CHAPTER 2 - Garden in Greenhouse 19
   Garden greenhouse cultivation for small spaces 20
   Greenhouses Features 22
CHAPTER 3 - Greenhouse Types 25
   Climate control 26
   Thermal accumulation in the ground 28
   Lighting 33
   Growing Techniques with Rfid Technology 33
CHAPTER 4 - How to Design a Greenhouse 35
   Supporting Structure 35
   Greenhouse Coverage 36
   Other useful tips and tricks 37
   Low-tech Greenhouses 37
   Mid-Tech Greenhouses 38
   Hi-Tech Greenhouses 38
CHAPTER 5 - Building a Do-It-Yourself Greenhouse ... 41
      Choice of Location 42
      Choice of Structure Type 43
      Choice of Covering Material 45
      Building of the Structure 46
      Check Temperature 48
      Additional Design 49
CHAPTER 6 - The Effects of Greenhouse Growth on the Environment 51
   Increasing Sustainability. 53
CHAPTER 7 - Planting Schedules to Promote Year-Round Growth 55
   What to Grow in the Cold Greenhouse? 55

CHAPTER 8 - Seeding guide 61
Why sow in Seedbeds? 61
- What types of veggies are appropriate for the seedbed? 62
- Buy or build the structure 63
- Seedbed characteristics 64
- Seedbed position 64
- Heating 65

What does it take to sow? 65
- Plant Containers 66
- Which soil to use? 66

How to plant the seedlings? 67
- When to sow the different species 68

After sowing 69
- Irrigations in the seedbed 69

When the seedlings are to be transplanted 70

CHAPTER 9 - Transplantation, Germination, and Sowing 73
Seeding Techniques 73
- Germination 76
- Seed quality 82

Plant Transplanting 82
- Production of plants intended for transplanting 84

CHAPTER 10 - How to Control Atmospheric Temperature and Humidity 89
Atmospheric Humidity 89

Temperature 91

Watering 92

CHAPTER 11 - Pests and Diseases 95
Vegetable Diseases and Pests 95
- Precautions when using agrochemicals 96
- Pesticides and Fungicides 97
- Methods of application 97

Plant Diseases 98

Vermin 104

CONCLUSION **111**

Kevin S. Stevenson
Greenhouse Gardening For Beginners

INTRODUCTION

Congratulations on buying this book and thank you for doing so. This book is designed specifically for those who want to build their own greenhouse and grow their own 100% organic vegetables and fruits to eat healthily and benefit their health.

Greenhouse cultivation is part of the concept of protected cultivation.

Would you like to learn more about this branch of agriculture and how to create a greenhouse?

The forms of cultivation in which means are used to protect plants from adverse climatic factors, which could affect their normal development, are called protected crops.

Protected crops include horticulture, floriculture, nursery and fruit-growing.

The means of protection include a very wide range of structures, which may differ:

Complexity: from simple ground cover to the most modern and complex greenhouses equipped with air conditioning systems.

For the duration of their use in relation to the cultivation cycle: i.e. the protection can be used for the entire cultivation period or only part of it.

With the use of the greenhouse it is possible:

- Realize a different degree of climate control.

- Cultivate certain species in environments other than those of origin where they can grow naturally (e.g. ornamental species of tropical origin cultivated in our environments).
- Anticipate or delay production compared to the normal period (semi-fortification).
- To realize productions completely out of season (forcing).

To obtain the forcing we use stable greenhouses: practicable structures equipped with glass or plastic covers and used for the whole cycle.

For the cultivation of plants in a sub-optimal environment and for semi-forced production, simpler means of protection such as agro-textiles or tunnels are enough.

The purpose of this book is particularly aimed at those who want to cultivate natural organic products at any time of the year both professionally and amateurishly.

This book will not only explain how to build your greenhouse but will also explain in detail which plants you can produce in your greenhouse, when to sow, how to maintain and care for the greenhouse and the plants to obtain excellent natural products.

This book will explain the complete processes and reasons for doing things in the specific ways that are recommended. It will give you a thorough understanding of the whole process from sowing to harvesting.

This book is a sincere attempt to help you understand the principles of greenhouse cultivation and the ways in which it can help you get genuine products and improve your health.

I hope you will be able to take full advantage of this book.

There are many books on this topic on the market, thank you again for choosing this one! Every effort has been made to ensure that it is full of as much useful information as possible; enjoy it!

Kevin S. Stevenson
Greenhouse Gardening For Beginners

CHAPTER 1 - Types of Greenhouses

When it comes to greenhouses, our mind almost always runs fast to the intensively cultivated fields. An image that doesn't really coincide entirely with what greenhouses are. A greenhouse, in fact, is an artificial environment that contributes to the growth of plants in environments not congenial to their cultivation. When we talk about plants, of course, we are not only referring to fruit plants or vegetables, but also to flowers. In this sense, there are numerous possibilities of application, which often have distant origins.

A brief historical note

The story of the greenhouses, in fact, starts from afar. The idea of growing in a protected environment spread when the passion for tropical plants was born, especially in northern countries. At that point it was necessary to identify systems that would allow plants to survive even in environments that were not congenial to their growth. According to some, already in the fifteenth century the first systems, such as the matted pavilions that allowed the growth of such plants, spread.

In the following centuries the passion for exotic plants and the spread of greenhouses grew in parallel. Already in the 18th century, in fact, you can recognize the first real greenhouses: not yet in the form to which we are accustomed today, but as buildings with large glass surfaces and colonnades to support them. The use of greenhouses, up to that point, was not limited only to the growth of plants. Greenhouses were, on the contrary, places to spend time and, for this purpose, were set up for banquets and dances.

With technological progress, iron replaced masonry colonnades. Thus, were born the winter gardens, which continued to be ornament of villas and palaces. Here too, however, the greenhouses have retained their function as halls to host parties. At the same time, however, the first experimental gardens became widespread, where plants that usually grow far away could be studied closely. From here to the use of greenhouses in cultivation, as we are used to nowadays, the step was short.

Types of greenhouses

The criteria for classifying greenhouse types are different. Essentially the different types of greenhouses can be grouped according to the function for which they are intended. In this case we can have:

- **multiplication greenhouses** (also called propagation greenhouses): they are greenhouses mainly used to promote the growth of roots in flowering and fruit plants.
- **forcing greenhouses** (also called cultivation greenhouses): these are greenhouses used for the cultivation of flowering and leafy plants, in order to promote their growth.
- **cultivation greenhouses**: these are the classic greenhouses used for the cultivation of garden plants.

- **drying greenhouses**: these are greenhouses which, as the definition itself states, are intended for the drying of agricultural products.

Greenhouses can also be classified according to their purpose. In that case we shall have them:

- **greenhouses for horticulture** (also called garden greenhouses): are greenhouses that are used for the cultivation of vegetables, which tend to be made of metal and plastic.
- **greenhouses for flowers** (also called greenhouses for floriculture): these are the greenhouses typically used for the cultivation of flowers.
- **garden greenhouses** (sometimes combined with ornamental greenhouses): these are greenhouses smaller than the usual ones, which allow even those who do not have large spaces, to grow their plants in greenhouses; their arrangement in the house, or in the garden of the house, means that the aesthetic care of this type of greenhouse is superior; also for this reason, especially indoor greenhouses, are also called ornamental greenhouses.
- **A particular type of greenhouse**, suitable for the cultivation of the winter garden, is the tunnel greenhouse. These are small greenhouses, which protect the vegetables during the coldest period of the year, without taking up much space.

From a constructive point of view, we recognize the existence of two types of greenhouses:

- **Double-pitched greenhouses**: These structures have asymmetrical and symmetrical pitches and are intended to produce flowers, succulents, vegetables and other crops. To encourage the passage of air, we suggest the installation of motorized openings. On this type of greenhouse, it is possible to install photovoltaic panels to support the environment.
- **Tunnel greenhouses** with semi-circular or elliptical vault: these structures are intended for the cultivation of tree crops and protected grapes. The materials generally used are polyethylene film. Also, in this case it is possible to install motorized or manual openings on the sides.

Temperature is also a peculiar feature of some greenhouses.

- **Cold greenhouses**: when they are not air-conditioned
- **Temperate greenhouses**: in this case the temperature is kept between 10 and 14°.
- **Hot greenhouses**: in this case the temperature can reach between 16° and 20°. If it exceeds 22° it will recreate a tropical climate.

Agrotextiles

Agro-textiles are means with an antifreeze or semi-freezing function. They are very large sheets of plastic, very light, which is placed over the crop without any support. This allows the plants to grow normally without any hindrance (at least up to certain limits).

The most common agro-textiles are permeable sheets made of polyester or pressed polypropylene fibre (called "non-woven fabric"), elastic and light. Their weight is about 17 g per square metre.

They are mainly suitable for autumn-winter or spring leaf vegetables: lettuce, chicory, radicchio, spinach.

Hydroponic greenhouses

Another type of greenhouse, which requires a separate chapter, are hydroponic greenhouses. These are greenhouses that exploit the principles of hydroponic cultivation. This type of cultivation does not use the soil, but only the water and nutrients necessary for plant development. This produces advantages, especially about the spread of certain plant diseases. In addition, by providing nutrients to the plant in a controlled manner, it is possible to modify the characteristics of its fruit. The hydroponic greenhouse, therefore, is a particular greenhouse that is based precisely on these principles. Many companies are trying to invest in this field, convinced that they can benefit from this type of cultivation.

Kevin S. Stevenson
Greenhouse Gardening For Beginners

CHAPTER 2 - Garden in Greenhouse

Cultivating is a passion that is often associated with the use of the greenhouse, if you want to have products always at hand or varieties that in cold weather would not survive in the open air.

There are many different types of greenhouse, knowing them will help us to understand which is best suited to our needs and our possibilities, not only economic, but also space. The choice also depends on what use we intend to make of them.

The most widespread and requested type of greenhouse is the economic and practical one. It is available on the market distributed in assembly kits, practical and quick to assemble, it takes about ten minutes. It costs little and is suitable for those who begin to try their hand at growing.

Usually the cheap greenhouse is suitable for those who have few vegetables and no aesthetic pretension, but simply seeks the essentiality of its function. This greenhouse can be disassembled and stored indoors after use, to be reassembled when it is needed again.

If you have never had to deal with a greenhouse, start with the cheap and practical greenhouse, it will help you to get familiar with this new way of growing vegetable garden and it will be a good training to then move on to other types of greenhouses, more demanding in maintenance and after all you can always reuse this greenhouse, since it is made to be assembled and reassembled in a few minutes.

Garden greenhouse cultivation for small spaces

Another type of greenhouse is the mini, perfect for those who do not have a large garden, but grow near the entrance of the house, in a small portion of land. The mini greenhouse is an easy, cheap and quite fast solution. You can find it in different materials: wood, metal or plastic. The choice of material also implies a difference in price.

The plastic mini greenhouse costs less than those made of wood or metal. The wooden ones are, however, the most popular, because they look like miniature closets that decorate the garden.

The mini greenhouse is a self-supporting structure leaning against it, divided into three zones, each with its own function. In the lower part the tools are stored together with fertilizer and soil (even if this area is often missing in the mini greenhouses, as in the one in the photo). In the central and upper part are placed the plants. Usually the central part is wide, for the taller plants, while in the upper part, aroma plants are placed.

Another type of greenhouse is the Victorian. The Victorian greenhouse is made of glass and metal, with doors and windows. It can be realized starting from the ground, as if it were a closed veranda, or using a lower part made of bricks, to reduce the cost of construction. The Victorian greenhouse is large, suitable for storing ornamental plants, but also for growing vegetables in winter, making the seedbed and storing tools and materials.

More than a greenhouse is considered an appendage of the house, where you can sit and chat with friends in cases where the space allows you to place a table with chairs inside it.

Finally, we have the pavilion greenhouse but one of the most fascinating.

The pavilion greenhouse has a hexagonal shape, built in wood and glass on a concrete base, with large windows on the sides and in some cases also on the roof, to allow more ventilation to the plants.

Greenhouses Features

Greenhouses are structures that respond to specific characteristics to ensure the right habitat for plants, flowers and vegetables.

Whatever their configuration, we start from the base. The floor must be of good quality for proper thermal insulation. The humidity must be kept at bay, so the floor must be solid and resistant.

Today most structures are made of steel, while the roof can be made of glass or plastic materials.

Glass is certainly much more resistant and lasts longer. In addition, it is often treated with metal oxides, so that unnecessary heat loss is avoided.

As far as plastic is concerned, polycarbonate (very common), PVC or reinforced polyester resins (typical of tunnel greenhouses) are used.

Air recirculation openings must be provided on the sides, especially during the summer season.

The door must be easy and comfortable, wide enough to allow the passage of tools and various materials.

Externally the presence of gutters or rainwater collection systems is recommended. In this way you can reduce the waste of water for irrigation.

Kevin S. Stevenson
Greenhouse Gardening For Beginners

CHAPTER 3 - Greenhouse Types

As mentioned before, from a constructive point of view, greenhouses are essentially of two types:

- **double-pitched**, with symmetrical or asymmetrical pitches whose use is the production of vegetables, flowers, succulent plants, mushrooms and any other type of crops To improve ventilation inside the greenhouse it is possible to install, near the ridge and on the sides, motorized openings with movement by means of racks. This type of structure is suitable for mounting photovoltaic modules on the roof thanks to the adequate inclination of the pitches that allows the right incidence of sunlight on the photovoltaic panels.

- **a tunnel,** with semi-circular or elliptical vault whose use is the production of vegetables, flowers, mushrooms, tree crops and protected grapes. The covering and the perimeter covering are in polyethylene film, stretched on the structure by means of a roller winding system. In addition, depending on requirements, they can also be made with other types of plastic materials available on the market. In particular cases, to improve the ventilation of the environment it is possible to install motorized or manual openings near the eaves.

Climate control

Air conditioning a greenhouse means controlling not only the temperature but also the relative humidity, ambient light and air exchange.

The equipment of an air conditioning system in a greenhouse is fundamental to ensure the maintenance of the ideal temperature and humidity for plant growth.

In hot and temperate greenhouses, heating is the most important component. Not being enough the greenhouse effect to ensure the temperature, artificial heating is almost always indispensable.

It is generally obtained with unit heaters, i.e. hot air generators equipped with fans.

The most common type for heating air is the suspended type that blows hot air into a perforated plastic film pipe, which is also suspended.

For the heating of the growing substrate, instead, PVC pipes positioned inside the substrate or on the bottom of the pallet are used. In the cultivation on the ground, the pipes must be buried in one depth of 20-30 cm.

During the summer period the greenhouse effect creates problems of overheating, so it is necessary to cool the greenhouse. Using the combined effect of shading and natural or forced ventilation.

There are also systems that exploit the evaporation of water to produce cooling and that do not require shading.

These are called "cooling system" and "fog system".

- The "cooling system" consists of fans placed on a wall and a battery of humidifying honeycomb panels placed on the opposite wall. The fans, having to guarantee a frequent air change, have high flow rates and are chosen and positioned in such a way as to draw air at low speed from the humidifier panels. The quantity of water to be dosed on the panels is around 2 litres per m2 of panel.
- The "fog system" consists in the diffusion in the greenhouse of water sprayed at high pressure (35-40 bar) by nozzles mounted on pipes placed above the crop. The entire operating system of the modern greenhouses (shading screens, mechanized openings and closures, thermal regulation, etc.) can be managed entirely by computer based on the inputs transmitted by sensors and peripheral microprocessors.

Among the facilities on the market we can list:

- HEATING PLANTS: with the use of hot air or hot water generators (in case of above ground cultivation) powered by oil or solid fuels.
- SHADDING PLANTS: the use of shading fabrics allows to reduce the volume of air to be heated in order to reduce energy consumption. The sheets can be placed horizontally inside the greenhouse at eaves height, and their movement can be automated with the use of light and temperature sensors.

Ultimately, all systems can be fully automated by installing automatic control units connected to temperature, humidity and other necessary sensors.

Thermal accumulation in the ground

As is well known, temperatures in the soil are more constant than in the air and less affected by external climatic variations as the depth increases. These considerations have suggested the development of systems suitable for temperature stabilization in greenhouses based on forced air circulation inside corrugated pipes placed in the soil.

During the summer period the outside air entering the pipes at the fan is warmer than the ground.

As it passes through the underground pipes, it transfers its heat to the ground and comes out cooler and can cool the greenhouse. At the same time the ground heats up.

This technique has an interesting possibility of application in greenhouses in cold season.

The system involves the recirculation of the greenhouse air, with the accumulation of heat in the ground during the day and the return of heat during the night, with the result of keeping the temperature of the greenhouse higher during the night.

The system can be improved by providing accumulation systems consisting, for example, of tanks with a certain volume of water placed in the ground and crossed by air pipes.

Growing Techniques

Depending on the growing technique, a distinction should be made between greenhouses with soil cultivation and greenhouses with above-ground cultivation.

- **Soil cultivation.** Soil cultivation in a protected environment can be on the ground or on pallets. Pallets are normally made for ornamental plants and cultivation is done on natural or artificial substrates. They can be fixed or mobile. The fixed ones are generally made of prefabricated metal or concrete structures and are 1.6-2 m wide. The surface area used, given the need to leave the passageways free, hardly exceeds 75 % of that covered. The mobile pallets, due to the need for lightness and corrosion resistance, are generally made of aluminium. They have the same dimensions as fixed pallets but, since they can be moved on rollers, the passage lane is not fixed but is created from time to time: this increases the usable surface area. Suspended pallets are also used; a solution that allows to have a surface used even more than 100% of the covered one. So-called "banquettes" are also used in ground cultivation. The ground of the greenhouse is divided into areas delimited by concrete slabs 20-30 cm high in order to create "beds" of cultivation width equal to or greater than one meter. Between one area and another, as with fixed pallets, there are lanes of passage. Unlike pallets, the growing substrate is not separated from the soil. Insulation can be achieved by placing a plastic film on the bottom and ensuring the drainage of irrigation water.

- **Growing above ground**. In greenhouses with above ground cultivation the most common form is based on the use of an inert and porous material (perlite, vermiculite, expanded clay, coconut fibre, pumice, etc.) as a substrate, on which a previously prepared nutrient solution is passed. Depending on the recovery of the nutritive solution, a distinction is made between closed and open cycle. Above ground crops represent a significant innovation introduced in the protected crops sector in recent years. Currently in Italy the technique is still not very widespread, involving about 7% of the entire surface area in protected crops, while in countries such as the Netherlands the percentage incidence exceeds 50%. Despite the advantage that this technique offers, especially in the management of mineral nutrition (also through software developed for this purpose that helps to calculate the amount of soluble salt to dissolve in water) and also in the greater control of diseases, above ground crops are difficult to spread, both for lack of cultivation of melons above ground and for the greater initial investment they require.

In the management of the nutrient solution, in addition to its chemical composition, the parameters to be kept under control are:

- the pH, which must be kept within an established range in order not to compromise the solubility of the nutrients and the exchange between the root system and the solution itself.
- the electrical conductivity, on which the control of the concentration of the nutritive solution depends (a low conductivity indicates an excessive dilution of the solution, while a high conductivity is equivalent to a high concentration and an excessive osmotic tension).
- the dispensing cycle and flow rates, from which the overall control of the mineral nutrition through the replacement of the solution is derived. Solution turnover requires careful management, especially for closed loop above ground crops. Management that, in order to be accurate, can only be computerized with dedicated software and based on calculation models related to the growth of the crop, the water consumption of the solution concentration, the salinity within the substrate.

On these aspects the research is very active, as well as the influence of the type of substrate and container of the same. A simplified hydroponic system developed at the beginning of the 1970s in England ("Nutrient Film Technique", NTF) involves the use of channels with an inclination of 1-1.5% protected at the top by an opaque plastic roof.

The pre-cultivated seedlings on inert materials (perlite, rock wool) are placed on the gutter in which the nutrient solution flows in a thin and continuous layer. In this way the roots are wetted by a veil of solution that is always in motion so there is no need to artificially aerate the solution.

Naturally, the nutrient solution is circulated by means of a pump with continuous control of pH and thermal conductivity.

Advantages of off-ground cultivation in peat or coconut fibre and perlite:

- increased production due to higher crop density (plants per linear metre).
- longer flowering time.
- fruit of constant size and homogeneous, high quality.
- optimisation of costs and working time, with a reduction in labour.
- protection of root systems from temperature changes thanks to the insulating power of expanded perlite.
- minimisation of risks of pests and pathogens.

Perlite is an effusive volcanic rock of variable colour between grey and pink, whose chemical composition is like that of rhyolites and dacite. Perlite can expand its volume up to 20 times its original volume when brought to high temperatures, close to its softening point. The expansion is linked to the presence of water that remains confined in the closed porosity of the rock as a result of the sudden cooling during the magma's escape.

When subjected to temperatures between 550 and 900° C, the rock expands due to the vaporization of the water: in this irreversible process bubbles are generated inside the granules of the bubbles that give the expanded rock the exceptional lightness that characterizes it, an extraordinary power of thermal insulation and the typical white colour.

Lighting

In Northern Europe, the reduced number of hours of daily lighting during the winter period severely limits the plant's growth possibilities. Artificial lighting is thus used. The electrical power normally installed is in the order of 50 W/m2.

Since a large part of the electrical energy is converted into heat, artificial lighting also contributes to heating.

Fluorescent lamps are mostly used, while incandescent lamps are not recommended because of their high consumption and the red-light band emitted unsuitable for plant growth.

Growing Techniques with Rfid Technology

In the Netherlands, the Walking Plant System (WPS), one of the leading suppliers of greenhouse management systems in the Netherlands, uses technology provided by companies specialising in the automatic identification of goods and

people and in the development of software, by marking each individual flowerpot with a transponder (tag), the entire greenhouse cultivation process has been optimised. With this project, WPS has demonstrated how the use of Rfid (Radio Frequency Identification) technology can also be used in greenhouses. The system developed by integrating Rfid technology with image technology is fully automated throughout the entire life cycle of the plant, from sowing to sale to the end customer.

The management software ensures that each plant can receive a specific treatment, according to its needs. Thanks to Rfid technology also the sales management is automated with great reliability.

CHAPTER 4 - How to Design a Greenhouse

When you worry about building a greenhouse, you must take into account that the materials to be used must be used for two different purposes: the first is to support the structure and therefore have a load-bearing function, the second is to convey heat, so you must choose a material that does not shield the construction too much.

Supporting Structure

Since their introduction, greenhouses are made of wood, a very economical material that can give some problems in the long run, breaking easily and changing with temperature changes.

To avoid major damage, if you have a higher budget, steel is certainly a good alternative: more resistant and less bulky than wood, this material is also useful to reduce heat loss.

However, the best choice for the supporting structure should be aluminium as it is extremely resistant. The only problem is its cost, certainly higher than the other alternatives.

Finally, if the greenhouse is small, plastic can also be a good option for the supporting structure.

Greenhouse Coverage

The strength of the greenhouse, as we explained in the previous lines, lies in its ability to store heat and this peculiarity depends on the type of material used for the roofing.

The choice of the right material is therefore essential and, bearing in mind that it must be transparent and able to filter light, there are various alternatives available:

- simple and polished glass
- raw glass, printed glass
- hammered glass
- striped glass

plastic with rigid, corrugated or smooth resin, polycarbonate or polyester sheets

As far as glass is concerned, there are many advantages to be listed because it is a transparent material, which resists humidity well and has a very high thermal insulation capacity; among the disadvantages there are certainly its heaviness and potential fragility.

Plastic, on the other hand, is decidedly lighter than glass and this will make it possible to choose less consistent (and cheaper) load-bearing structures; at the same time, plastic does not have the same level of transparency as glass, which could compromise the ultimate goal of the construction of the greenhouse itself.

Other useful tips and tricks

In order to avoid that all the work done to build the greenhouse is in vain, it is right to carry out thermal insulation work that will be able to minimize the internal heat loss.

This process involves the application of horizontal sheets of transparent polyethylene bubble on the outside of the structure; to fix them correctly, an air vacuum must be created between the vacuum and the roof.

In a greenhouse it is essential to organize the internal space in a rational and efficient way so that your work is as easy as possible.

The insertion of a worktable and metal pallets can help you achieve this, allowing you to position crops according to their need for sunshine.

Finally, don't forget to equip your greenhouse with water outlets, electrical sockets and artificial lights, one or more hot air generators, a thermometer and an automatic irrigation system.

Low-tech Greenhouses

For this type of greenhouses an investment of around 20-25 euros/m2 is required.

The structure is very simple, and the cover is made of plastic. The climate control is poor and often there is no heating system.

The species grown in these greenhouses are low-income vegetables and cut flowers. The cultivation technique is simple and does not differ much from that used in the open field. In the case of vegetables, these are often tunnel greenhouses.

Mid-Tech Greenhouses

For this type of greenhouses an investment of around 25-80 euro/m2 is required.

The structure is generally made of metal and both glass and plastic (often rigid panels) are used as covering material.

Climate control is more efficient than in the previous case and the internal environment is relatively independent from the external one; in the case of vegetables, however, they are often "cold greenhouses" (without heating or with emergency heating in case of frost).

Cultivation techniques are more advanced, and include hydroponic systems, with many partially or fully automated cultivation operations.

These greenhouses are used not only for growing vegetables out of season, but also for high value cut flowers (example rose) and potted ornamental plants.

Hi-Tech Greenhouses

For this type of greenhouses, the investment required is more than 80 euros/m2 and can reach or even exceed 160 euros/m2.

Generally, the supporting structure is made of galvanized iron and the covering material is glass. You have a sophisticated climate control, based on:

- heating of both the air and the root zone
- forced ventilation
- cooling and humidification systems (e.g. cooling system)
- light conditioning (artificial lighting and shading)
- carbon enrichment

The indoor climate can be completely independent of the outdoor climate. Cultivation systems are designed to maximise the efficiency of space use and minimise the use of labour.

These greenhouses are mainly used for the cultivation of ornamental plants and to produce propagation material in cold climate regions.

Kevin S. Stevenson
Greenhouse Gardening For Beginners

CHAPTER 5 - Building a Do-It-Yourself Greenhouse

The construction of a greenhouse is a demanding project; however, it can be carried out economically or perhaps by relying on professional builders.

Things you will need

- Mounting kit for greenhouses
- Tape measure
- Wooden beams
- Gravel
- Glass panels
- Glass fibre panels
- Double-walled plastic sheets
- PVC
- Iron rod
- Wire
- Stakes
- Wood treatment products
- Fans
- Thermometers
- Electric, wood or gas heating elements
- Breathers
- Cisterns
- Water
- Aiuole
- Tables for vases

Choice of Location

Choose an area with a southern exposure. The first requirement for a greenhouse is always to be exposed to plenty of sunshine.

All structures should be located north of the greenhouse.

A rather common form of construction for greenhouses is the one leaning against another building. In this case it is good to choose a south facing wall.

Places that are exposed to the sun in the morning rather than in the evening are preferable. The best option is always to have the sun all day long, but if this is not possible, exposure to the sun in the morning is more conducive to plant growth.

If there are trees or shrubs in the vicinity of the greenhouse, make sure they do not shine on the greenhouse until late afternoon.

Consider winter sunshine compared to summer sunshine. If the area facing east is open and sunny, you will get better sunshine from November to February.

The sun's rays in winter have less inclination, so trees, houses and other structures can cause more shade problems.

Do not choose a location near evergreen trees. Decaying trees lose their leaves and get less shade in winter, when the greenhouse needs more sun.

Choose a location where electricity is available. Many greenhouses require heating and ventilation to maintain the optimum temperature.

If you build a greenhouse against a house, you can get the energy you need through an extension of the house's electrical system.

Installing an electrical system in a separate building may require an electrician.

Choose an area with good drainage. You will need to drain the excess rainwater.

If the ground in the chosen area has hollows, you will probably need to fill them to improve drainage.

You can install rainwater tanks to collect rainwater from the roof of the greenhouse. Every form of saving water and energy supply helps to reduce the operating costs of the greenhouse.

Choice of Structure Type

Measure the available space. Whether you decide to build the greenhouse from scratch or with the help of an assembly kit, choose your dimensions carefully.

The larger the greenhouse, the higher the costs for construction and heating.

You can easily find greenhouses in assembly kits with dimensions of 2x3x1.8 m, or 3x6x1.8 m.

Choose a greenhouse in kit, if you have little experience in construction or if you do not have someone who can help you.

You can buy a small polycarbonate greenhouse in a mounting box at DIY stores or online at Amazon or eBay, starting from just over $60.

You can find larger and more robust models from $450 and up, depending on the size.

In addition to generic websites, you can look at the sites of chains that specialize in selling gardening materials.

Build a wall mounted greenhouse. If you have chosen an area adjacent to a building, you can build a simple structure against a wall.

If the wall is made of brick or concrete, the warmth of the building itself can help maintain a constant warmth.

This is a very simple structure that you can build yourself. You can build it with iron rods, tubulars, wooden beams; in general, it will need less support elements than a stand-alone construction.

Build a tunnel greenhouse. This is a type of greenhouse with a tunnel roof, which can be built with steel supports or PVC pipes.

The tunnel shape means less space in height and reduced storage capacity compared to rectangular models.

This type can be built with little expense; however, the cheapest materials are also generally the least robust.

Choose a rigid structure. For this type you will need to build foundations and a supporting structure. Unless you are an expert in building design, we recommend that you commission the project from a specialist or delegate the construction to someone else.

A rigid structure, made with support poles and beams, requires foundations and strong structural elements.

To build a large rigid greenhouse you will need the help of friends or professional bricklayers.

Choice of Covering Material

Uses polyethylene film for greenhouses, UV treated. The light transmission is like that of glass, but it is light and inexpensive.

The plastic film should be renewed after a few years.

It needs to be washed from time to time.

It does not retain heat as well as glass, but it is suitable for wall and tunnel greenhouses, and for small rigid greenhouses.

It uses rigid double-walled plastic material.

Polycarbonate lends itself to being slightly curved and allows energy savings of up to 30% thanks to the double wall.

It typically allows 80% of the light to pass through.

Choose glass fibre. If you want to build a rigid greenhouse, you can save money by using fibreglass instead of glass.

Choose transparent fiberglass.

You will need to restore the resin cover every 10-15 years.

You prefer high quality fiberglass. The light transmission is much lower in the case of low-quality glass.

Choose glass. This is the most beautiful material to see, if you intend to build a greenhouse to decorate your house or garden.

Glass is very fragile, and repairs are expensive.

You must necessarily build a greenhouse with a rigid structure with a foundation.

Tempered glass is preferable because it is more resistant than ordinary glass.

If you intend to pay the cost of installing a glasshouse, we recommend that you ask for offers from specialist builders to ensure that the foundation and structure are adequate to support the weight.

Building of the Structure

Tension wires on the ground to measure the position of the supports. Plant stakes in the ground.

Create iron rod reinforcements. If you are building a greenhouse against a wall or a tunnel greenhouse, you can create the structure with rod and PVC.

Plant the rods in the ground at a regular distance of 120 cm. Let it protrude about 120 cm.

Once the rods are in place, make arches from side to side with 6 m long PVC pipe sections. Spread the polyester sheet over the arch structure and fix it at the bottom to joists.

Pour gravel on the ground to form a homogeneous layer, after planting the supports in the ground. The use of well melted fine gravel promotes excellent drainage of the greenhouse.

If you need foundations, have masons do the work. They will assemble formwork and cast the greenhouse floor before the structure can be built.

Apply a protective treatment to all wooden parts before you put them in place.

Untreated wood rots within 3 years.

Choose carefully the type of treatment for the wooden parts. The use of certain treatment products does not allow the food produced to be considered "organic" due to the chemical compounds they contain.

Some wood treatment products are specifically designed to reduce leaching. Leaching is the process by which soluble elements of the soil are transported or migrate into the deeper layers as a result of water flow and percolation.

It is better to prefer metal support elements rather than wooden ones.

Seal the roof over the structure as well as possible. In the case of plastic film, you can fix it to the wood with bolts.

The more expensive the roofing material is, the more care you will have to take when sealing the roof connections to the foundations and the supporting structure.

Find out the best way to apply the cover you have chosen.

Check Temperature

Place fans in the corners of the greenhouse. Place them diagonally.

They should be on most of the time throughout the winter to ensure a homogeneous temperature throughout the greenhouse.

Install vents in the greenhouse ceiling. You can also place them near the top of the supports.

A certain degree of carbon dioxide ventilation is essential.

The vents should be adjustable. You will need to open them more in the summer months.

Consider installing an electric heating system. Depending on the climate, exposure to sunlight can contribute as little as 25% to heating. In these cases, some additional heating is indispensable.

You can also use a wood or kerosene stove, but this solution requires the installation of a chimney to ensure good air quality.

You should contact the municipal technical office to check which types of heating are allowed in your area.

Install an air conditioning system if yours is a glass-walled greenhouse. If you can afford to install a temperature control system you can grow practically anything.

Have a professional electrician install the system.

The system will require regular maintenance to ensure ventilation and heating during the winter.

Install thermometers or thermostats. Install more than one thermometer in case one fails.

Place them at different heights in the greenhouse.

You can install a thermometer that transmits the temperature measurement to a display inside the house, so you can comfortably keep an eye on the temperature of the greenhouse during the winter months.

Additional Design

Study the environmental conditions required by the plants you intend to grow. The more sensitive a species is to temperature and humidity conditions, the less likely it is to grow other species in the same area.

A cold greenhouse is a greenhouse designed to prevent plants from freezing. It is ideal as temporary protection.

A warm greenhouse is a greenhouse suitable for tropical plants.

Choose the desired temperature and keep it constant. It is not possible to create zones with different temperatures unless separating walls are installed.

Make sure you have adequate water availability. Ideally it should be water for irrigation or from tanks.

Build raised flowerbeds inside the greenhouse. You can also use tables with perforated shelves to help drain water.

If possible, build flowerbeds considering the height of the grower for ergonomic reasons.

CHAPTER 6 - The Effects of Greenhouse Growth on the Environment

Greenhouse cultivation causes a high environmental impact, which is expressed in:

- Defacement of the landscape and increase in the area of sealed soil.
- Waste disposal (roofing and other plastic materials, substrates, drainage solutions, etc.).
- Greenhouse gas emissions (heating systems).
- Intensive use of chemical products (fertilisers, pesticides, geopharmaceuticals, weed killers, herbicides, plant growth regulators) and water (often not of good quality). This causes problems of soil salinization, groundwater pollution, product contamination.
- Monoculture or in any case high crop specialization, thus causing a loss of biological "fertility" of soils due to accumulation of pathogenic organisms.

The area of Almeria, in Spain, is one of the most intensive in the world for the use of greenhouses. In Italy, Sicily is one of the regions with the highest number of greenhouses.

Data for Almeria are estimated annually:

- 1.1 t/ha of PE for roofing renewal (every 2-3 years)
- 112 kg/ha of plastic laces for plant tutoring
- 50 kg/ha of polypropylene colour traps for insects
- 500 kg/ha of plastic for irrigation systems and others, such as mulch residues, plastic coverings for greenhouse

coverings, polystyrene containers used in nurseries, off-ground substrate residues (sacks), etc.

In the Netherlands, in heated greenhouses, 800 t/ha per year of CO_2 is released compared to 200 t/ha per year of CO_2 equivalent fixed by the crop: this balance represents the environmental and extra-seasonal cost.

The agroecosystem greenhouse is considered among those with the highest consumption of pesticides. For the phytosanitary protection of crops, an average of 10 chemical treatments/cultivation is carried out, with peaks that can exceed 20 interventions/cultivation for some floricultural species.

The annual quantity of pesticides used in Italy in intensive sericulture production is 47 kg/ha (active ingredient), in the Netherlands, on the other hand, it is about 31 kg/ha.

Not infrequently farmers use an excess of water and fertilizers compared to the actual needs of the plants.

For example, the supply of fertilizers in a tomato greenhouse in Sicily is about 6 t/ha per year, but only a certain percentage of nutrients is absorbed by the crop.

Excessive nutrient inputs compared to plant uptake result in problems of groundwater pollution (especially N) and accumulation of salts in the soil.

Increasing Sustainability.

Problems	Possible solutions
Landscape impact	Structural constraints and regulation of the expansion of covered areas in areas of landscape value by public administrations.
Plastic Disposal	Use of biodegradable plastic (mulching, small tunnels), long-life film (3-4 years, large tunnels), glass (greenhouses). Recycling of plastic materials.
Substrate disposal	Use of substrates that can be used for several cycles (ease of disinfection) and/or recyclable (e.g. organic substrates: compost, biomass for energy production).
Drainage solutions	Closed" cultivation systems (with irrigation water < 1 ds/m)
Gas emissions	Choose species and cultivars with low thermal requirements. Take measures to reduce heat loss (heat shields). Use basal heating. Use alternative energy sources (e.g. organic residues) or renewable energy sources (solar, wind, biomass, etc.). Use the gases produced by heating for carbon enrichment of the greenhouse.

Soil salinization	Correct management of irrigation and fertilization. Rainwater harvesting.
Massive use of pesticides	Integrated and biological fight. Use of resistant cultivars. Steam disinfection;
Organic soil weariness	Adoption of long rotations. Off-ground cultivation systems. Use of resistant cultivars. Grafting on resistant rootstocks

CHAPTER 7 - Planting Schedules to Promote Year-Round Growth

What to Grow in the Cold Greenhouse?

In a cold greenhouse we can grow practically all vegetable garden crops, usually depending on the size you decide what to plant indoors and what to leave outdoors.

Among the most efficient plants to keep in the tunnel are salads, carrots, radish, beets and spinach. These plants take up little space and are well suited to spring and winter, offering good resistance to cold. Summer fruit vegetables such as solanaceae and cucurbitaceae are bulkier and require a greenhouse of good size.

Growing vegetables in the greenhouse is not very different from growing them in the open-air garden, but there are some significant differences. Firstly, the roofing not only protects against the cold but also limits the air circulation and protects against rain. This means that the grower must provide proper irrigation and airing the indoor space properly.

Very important is the choice of the position where to put our greenhouse: it must be sunny and easy to access for us.

Inside the greenhouse we can apply the same general principles valid for the outdoor garden: subdivision of the flowerbeds and walkways, arrangement of the drip system, mulching, sowing some flowers that attract pollinators and eco-friendly methods of fertilization and defence against adversity.

If the greenhouse is big enough, we can afford to keep at least the first meter of length as a space of movement, to support the tools, seeds and seedlings that we are going to use, to keep a service table, a chair, the bin full of water for irrigation, etc..

Period in which to use it

The cold greenhouse can be used practically all year round. Without any doubt, it is better to exploit it in full during the months of January-March in the south, February-April in the north, and also for the whole autumn, because these are precisely the periods in which having a greenhouse can make a great difference.

In this way, the production of spinach, various types of lettuces, chard, rocket and other vegetables can be prolonged.

When you go towards winter the greenhouse may still contain vegetables, but in periods when temperatures fall below zero it is good to cover them with non-woven cloth.

During the summer, on the other hand, very high temperatures can be generated inside the greenhouse and cultivation is only possible if the structure can be opened well on the sides. It may also be advisable to cover the roof of the greenhouse with shading nets in case of strong sunlight.

Inside the greenhouse (as mentioned above) we will have to provide irrigation, and for this purpose it certainly makes sense to set up a drip system, to encourage a gradual distribution of water without excesses.

However, it may be worthwhile to make sure to collect rainwater by fixing gutters along the long sides of the greenhouse, at the top, which will introduce the water that falls on the greenhouse in drums below. If the greenhouse is small, we can also irrigate manually by filling the watering can with water from these bins. It is useful to keep other bins full inside the greenhouse, to let the water cool down for some time before using it.

Sloping roof greenhouses usually have windows at the sides and/or on the roof, in addition to the doors, while tunnels generally offer the possibility of opening the sides.

When choosing a prototype greenhouse, it is advisable to take this into account, because during the hot hours of the day it is important to open the greenhouses to circulate air and disperse moisture, which favours the onset of fungal diseases.

In the long run, the cover of the greenhouse can become dirty and opaque, limiting the entry of light, and if there are trees nearby, it is possible that leaves may accumulate on the upper part. As a result, periodic cleaning is always necessary to ensure good lighting efficiency indoors.

With a small structure of about 2 x 3 m or 2 x 4 m we can already obtain some discreet family productions, but if possible it is better to choose a larger one, for example a tunnel measuring 3 x 10 m, which can allow us to diversify the crops and give us satisfaction.

However, in general it makes sense to relate the size of a greenhouse to the total area of the garden, considering the uncovered crops and the space they require.

A large greenhouse also allows us to allocate part of the surface area to the seedbed activity to produce seedlings and cuttings of perennial species, and this is also an interesting aspect.

For good ventilation, the greenhouse should have two doors, or at least openable roofs and openings on the sides. Depending on the structure and the size, the methods for changing air will vary. In tunnels you usually lift the tarpaulin on the side.

Let's summarize what to grow in the greenhouse in winter

Here is a list of what you can grow in the unheated greenhouse in the middle of winter:

- salads,
- radishes,
- valerianella,
- spinach,
- onions,
- garlic,
- turnips,
- cabbages,
- chicory,
- radicchi,
- parsley,
- celery,
- carrots,
- fennel,
- Brussels sprouts,
- wild strawberries,
- tomatoes

Those who live in northern Italy should not dare to grow tomatoes under a greenhouse if they do not have a heated greenhouse. This is because the tomato could also lead to the production of fruits but, because of the cold, it would give you tomatoes that are not very juicy and have inadequate organoleptic properties.

Some recommended greenhouse models

- **Greenhouse Kenley** 3×2. Small and versatile tunnel greenhouse, with steel structure and roll-up tarpaulin.
- **Outsunny** greenhouse 4.5×2. Other tunnel model, slightly larger than Kenley, with iron tubular structure and ventilation windows.
- **Tunnel lock** 6×3. Larger size greenhouse, up to 2 meters high, with good value for money. Double door and good opening system with roll-up tarpaulin on the sides.
- **TecTake** greenhouse of 11 square meters, with aluminium structure and polycarbonate walls. A greenhouse beautiful to see, therefore suitable for vegetable garden contexts in the garden, equipped with door and windows on the sloping roof. The materials make it quite expensive.
- **Mini greenhouse Valmas**. Ingenious roofing system, very easy to place and well resistant. Suitable for quick interventions to protect the winter garden from unforeseen cold or spring crops in case of late frost.

Kevin S. Stevenson
Greenhouse Gardening For Beginners

CHAPTER 8 - Seeding guide

Most of the vegetables we know are not sown directly in the garden but are grown starting with transplanting.

The seedlings can be bought from nurseries or trusted shops, but learning how to get them on your own is a great step forward: it allows you to save money and to grow for each species just the varieties we are interested in, since the purchase of seed sachets can be organized in time and with a good choice compared to that of the ready seedlings.

By seedbed or nursery, we mean a transparent structure, usually covered with plastic sheets, glass or Plexiglas and whose function is to offer a warm microclimate to the plants growing inside.

Why sow in Seedbeds?

The advantages that the seedbed technique offers compared to direct sowing in the garden are various and interesting.

Select seedlings. First, we can sow more seedlings than those that are really needed in the garden, so when they are ready, we will have the possibility to choose the best and the most uniformly developed ones.

Optimize the space in the garden. With seedlings spending the first phase of their life in the seedbed, they keep the garden beds occupied for a shorter time, and these can be used for other crops beforehand. Think of all those species that are only transplanted at the end of April or May, for example pumpkins: if we sowed them directly in the garden we would have to do so at the beginning of April, and the space would then already be occupied a month earlier, perhaps not allowing spinach or salads to be grown on that same space previously.

Anticipate sowing. The seedbed is a sheltered place, where it is possible to sow a few weeks earlier than direct sowing, as the internal temperature is higher.

Less weeding work. You must consider that the transplanted seedlings have an advantage over the weeds, even if soon we will still have to intervene by hoeing or mulching.

Economic savings. Finally, there is the saving on the purchase of the seedlings, which will soon pay back the small initial investment to set up the structure.

What types of veggies are appropriate for the seedbed?

Even if most horticultural crops can be grown in seedbeds, it is important to know that some species do not tolerate transplanting, so it is good to know which crops are suitable for sowing in trays.

All cucurbits lend themselves very well to transplanting pumpkin, courgette, melon, watermelon and cucumber. The technique is also valid for pepper, chilli, aubergine, tomato, head lettuce, chard, celery, cabbage and other vegetables.

Usually, those species that are to be placed at well-defined distances in the garden are transplanted, while it would be less convenient for the species that are placed in a continuous row, such as rocket and parsley, or peas and beans, because in this way too many seedlings would be needed and therefore it would be better to sow directly in rows. Some farms, however, transplant rocket, spinach and parsley, because with the direct sowing in rows the rapid birth of weeds would then make it problematic to keep the row clean and therefore prefer to transplant the tufts of 3-4 seedlings on black perforated sheets.

For carrots, turnips and radishes transplanting is not recommended because the rooting of the seedlings is difficult, being a root species, it is better to sow directly in the garden, in order to obtain a more regular vegetable of good size.

If we have little space for the seedbed, we must make a choice between seedlings to sow and those to buy. In this case it is preferable to buy leek and onion seedlings because they are placed in the garden at short distances and you need a lot of them: we would risk investing all our small seedbed space only with these. In addition, leek and onion seeds can be stored for a maximum of 2 years, so if there are any open sachets left over, they may expire before they are fully used.

Buy or build the structure

If you practise carpentry and manual work amuses us, you can build a wooden or alternatively metal support structure yourself, which you can then cover with transparent material. The do-it-yourself seedbed is not difficult to do, the important thing is to provide convenient openings to perform all the necessary operations afterwards.

If we opt instead for the purchase of the seedbed greenhouse, the expense to buy it will still be amortized in a relatively short time, given the savings on the purchase of seedlings, you can choose from many different solutions that you find on the market, you must select the most suitable according to the size and characteristics.

Seedbed characteristics

As we have already seen the seedbed is a wooden or metal structure with walls and transparent cover (so glass, plastic sheet or plexiglass panels), we see that other characteristics must have as dimensions and positioning.

Seedbed position

In order to position our small greenhouse, you must prefer a sunny position but also sheltered from the winds. The seedbed can be placed directly in the vegetable garden but in this way, it takes away useful space for cultivation, so it is good to consider other sunny corners outside this area. Given the frequent care that seedlings require, it is essential that the seedbed is close to the place where you live or work, or alternatively have collaborations for daily care. In fact, the production of seedlings could be an important shared activity between several garden growers.

There are no limits to the size of a seedbed greenhouse, we must rely on the possibilities of space we have. Ideally the space to put the seedlings should be related to the surface of the garden. Usually a few square meters are enough, in which to exploit also the verticality with various shelves, if it is done without sacrificing light.

If the seedbed has the conformation of a real greenhouse for vegetable garden, however small, it is useful to put inside it one or more work tables that we need to do the sowing and then to keep all the containers lined up there. Obviously, if it is a small-scale seedbed, the work will be done outside, and no furniture is needed except the spaces where to put the sowing trays.

Heating

Having a heated seedbed can be very useful to advance sowing and earn a few weeks. A sheltered room with walls that let in light already tends to create a higher temperature than the room, but sometimes heating is useful. In order not to dissipate energy unnecessarily, it is better to heat a small seedbed to germinate the seeds. For this purpose, you can use cheap mats, we have gone into the article on how to heat the seedbed.

What does it take to sow?

Once the structure has been built, we'll get to work, so let's see what we need for sowing: from the pots to the soil, all the way to the seeds.

Plant Containers

For sowing we can start to keep all the black trays that were sold to us with the previous seedlings, but it may be necessary to buy others. The black colour of these trays has the function of rapidly heating the soil inside them and speeding up the birth of the seedlings. In theory you can sow in any small container of small size, piercing the bottom to avoid dangerous stagnation of excess water, in small scale you can use, for example, jars of recycled yoghurt, in practice, however, to optimize space is better to choose the classic trays for seedlings, which have a low cost and allow you to better organize the seedbed.

An environmentally sustainable alternative to classic plastic or polystyrene trays is the soil blocker system, which also has great advantages on the cultivation side.

Which soil to use?

For substrates it is good not to choose the classic universal potting soil, because it contains some coarse material, not functional to put small seeds in a jar. The professional potting soil for sowing is finer and therefore better, but over time we can also learn to use less potting soil by mixing it with soil and compost, both previously sieved.

A good recipe for producing your own seeding soil is to mix vegetable garden soil, silica sand and brown peat (you can make a third for each component). The use of earthworm humus in the substrate is also positive, as well as nourishing helps the rooting.

There are also some ready-made peat disks (like the ones you can find here), this is a much cheaper solution, although more convenient. Those who cultivate on the balcony can choose it for not having around bags of soil that dirty.

To grow an organic vegetable garden, you should choose seeds that come from organic farming, or at least have not been tanned with fungicides. Ideally it is also useful to learn how to preserve and reproduce the seeds of some vegetables, so this operation is simple, such as tomatoes and peppers.

How to plant the seedlings?

There are species with large seeds, such as zucchini and cucumbers, for which sowing is very simple. In each hole of the black trays, completely filled with soil, we can put a single seed from which a seedling will be born.

For species with small seeds, such as lettuces, cabbage, chicory or peppers, it is better to spread on the wet soil in a small bowl many seeds to be covered with a thin layer of soil passed through a sieve. So many seedlings will be born, and we will soon put them through a marking out, the technique that consists of gently extracting the seedlings and replant them in new containers with soil, each in its own compartment of tray. This operation must be done when the seedlings are very small and have a long but still little branched root. For the repicking we help ourselves with a stick to gently push the root of the seedling into the potting soil. The seedlings usually take root without problems and grow independently of each other, each with its own soil bread. There are also those who let them all grow together and separate them only at the time of transplanting, but usually the seedlings grown together look a bit spunky, because they have taken light away from each other.

Remember to put labels to indicate which vegetable you have sown in each jar; you can also make very pretty ones.

When to sow the different species

Among the first seedlings of the season that we are going to sow in the seedbed are head lettuces and Cataluña chicory, which are born at only 4 or 5 °C. Soon we can continue with chard, cabbage, borage and tomatoes, and when temperatures are mild, we sow cucurbits, pepper, basil and aubergine.

For autumn vegetables (all cabbage and various endives and chicory) we sow from June to July, while fennel is sown only in July and transplanted in August, because anticipating the sowing of fennel before June 21 exposes it to the risk of pre-flowering. To avoid this, in fact, the days must have started to shorten, and July is the most suitable period.

For these summer sowings, however, the seedbed must always remain open on the sides, acting at that point as a roof that protects the plants from thunderstorms and summer hailstorms.

For certain species sowing can be staggered and is a very recommended choice because it allows to obtain harvests distributed over time. Lettuce, chard, courgette, cucumber, cucumber, cabbage and leek are very suitable for sowing.

After sowing

Let's see what care needs to be taken in the seedbed after planting the seed, to encourage sprouting and then let the seedlings develop correctly.

Irrigations in the seedbed

The seedlings should be watered with the watering can equipped with a shower, for a gentle jet, you can also use a nebulizer. Watering does not have to be daily because it depends on the weather conditions. In spring there are very humid and still cold periods during which the soil of the plants does not dry every day, as well as very hot and sunny days during which it may be necessary to water twice a day. The only certain rules are to check and observe well the state of the soil and the seedlings and irrigate when necessary, preferring the cool hours of the day to do so.

Precautions

There are basically two precautions to be taken for the care of seedlings in seedbeds:

Water with water at room temperature, keeping a full container inside the seedbed or mixing the tap water so that it is warm. Cold water can in fact induce stress to the seedlings.

Air the seedbed during hot days, opening all the openings to circulate air and avoid condensation. In the evening, however, it is always good to close the structure.

Possible diseases and pests of the seedlings

The seedlings in the seedbed can be eaten by snails, so if there is any doubt that they can enter, it is better to distribute around the sowing containers some iron orthophosphate, a slug killer allowed in organic farming.

We can also note the onset of fungal diseases, favoured by the humid microclimate that is established in these environments, and among these we remember the pithium which, together with others, causes the death of the seedbeds. It is necessary to manage this inconvenience by treating with a product based on the antagonist fungus Thricoderma. If we manage to save the seedlings from the disease and transplant them, it will then be appropriate to disinfect the containers in which they have been immersed for a few hours in water and vinegar.

When the seedlings are to be transplanted

To understand when the seedlings are ready you need to make some observations and know the stage of those that are sold. The head lettuces and beets in general have formed at least 4 leaves, the tomatoes are about 15 cm tall, but the final proof is that extracting the soil block from the alveolus the roots hold it all and this does not crumble. If we see that the roots are all too wrapped and developed around the soil block this is a sign that we have waited longer and to confirm this we will notice that the seedling starts to yellow, because that soil is no longer sufficient. After transplanting it generally recovers, but it is always good not to get to this point.

From sowing to transplanting there is not always a defined time, because the germination and development of the seedlings are related to the temperature of the environment. Seedlings sown in February may arrive after a month and a half to transplant, while those sown in late spring are ready much earlier.

Once they are ready, the seedlings do not need to be transplanted immediately, but it is advisable to take them out of the greenhouse, keeping them still in the containers to acclimatize for a day or two, and only after transplanting them in the space we have chosen for them in the garden.

Kevin S. Stevenson
Greenhouse Gardening For Beginners

CHAPTER 9 - Transplantation, Germination, and Sowing

Seeding Techniques

In order to increase and improve the uniformity of sowing and germination for vegetable species characterized by small and irregular seeds (e.g. carrot, celery, endive, onion, etc.), techniques have been developed:

- Pelleting
- Calibration
- Pre-germination

Pelleting

Sugar coating of the seed consists in externally surrounding the seeds with different materials based on clay and/or vermiculite. Vermiculite facilitates germination of the seeds, which can occur even in less than optimal conditions of humidity. Other substances, such as pesticides, fertilisers and hormones, can also be mixed with the sugar-coating material.

Recently, another method of sugar coating, called split pills, has been developed. Through this system, the sugared material in contact with soil moisture detaches from the seed. However, however, it is necessary that the moisture is optimal to prevent the sugared material from sticking to the seed and causing burns to the seedlings.

The technique of sugared almonds has become particularly popular in precision seeding for small seed species (e.g. lettuce, chicory and endive).

Calibration

Calibration is a technique that consists of selecting the various types of seeds according to their size.

Among the advantages that this practice has, are:

- Simultaneity in germination and emergence of seedlings
- Tolerance to suboptimal temperatures
- Uniformity of growth of seedlings
- Possibility of using precision seed drills more efficiently
- Contemporary collection of the production.

The calibration technique has been developed not only for small seed species, but especially for many F1 hybrid cultivars.

For F1 hybrids, sizing and counting improves the use of the product, because they are higher cost seeds that are marketed according to their number and not according to their weight.

Pre-germination

Pre-germination is a technique that consists in reducing the germination and emergency period of the seedlings, through the simple and traditional system of seed moistening.

This system is widespread for vegetable species belonging to the Cucurbitaceae family (e.g. zucchini, pumpkin, watermelon and melon).

The seeds are immersed in warm water for about 24 to 48 hours and then transferred to a warm, dark environment in the presence of peat until the radicle is released. Once pre-germinated, the seeds are placed in jars and then planted in the greenhouse. This technique is particularly applied to early-cycle spring species in order to anticipate their germination.

Pre-germination has then been successfully extended also for direct sowing in open field in order to ensure regular and simultaneous germination even under unfavourable conditions.

In this case, germination is first carried out under favourable conditions, after which sowing is carried out using well equipped machines, which deposit the pre-germinated seed on a substrate that ensures the emergence of seedlings.

The methods that can be used are:

1) Pre-germination in gelatinous substrates (fluid drilling)

This method consists of distributing the pre-germinated seed in a gel-like substrate through an injection machine. The method is suitable for humid climates and clayey soils, as the gel rapidly disintegrates.

2) Pre-germination in solid substrates (plug mix)

This method, on the other hand, consists in having the seed pregerminated on a substrate based on peat and/or vermiculite to be followed by their localized distribution with specific machines.

In this sense, cubes of peat-based substrate are produced, containing 2 - 3 germinated seeds which are then spaced according to the required crop density so that the germination process can continue for a certain period even under unfavourable environmental conditions.

This method has been developed in Italy particularly for precision sowing of industrial tomatoes in environments that are not favourable to germination and for delayed sowing.

Germination

Seed germination is the sum of all the morphological, physiological and biochemical phases that seeds undergo in order to generate a new plant.

For the germination process to take place, four conditions must be met:

- The embryo of the seed is vital
- There must be no physiological, physical or chemical (dormancy) obstacles to the germination process.
- The environmental conditions (temperature and humidity) are favourable.

Germination must take place rapidly, both to limit the phase of permanence in the seedbed and to reduce the parasite attacks that can be caused by the seed and the new seedling.

The germination of seeds takes place in three very distinct phases which are:

- Phase 1: Awakening of the seed (activation).
- Phase 2: Digestion and distribution of seed substances.
- Phase 3: Development of the seedling.

Phase 1: Awakening of the seed can in turn be divided into three other sub-phases which are:

- Seed imbibition
- Synthesis of enzymes and hormones
- Rootle leak.

The seed imbibition phase is the one that occurs immediately after the seed has passed the dormancy phase.

In this phase, the seed becomes permeable to oxygen and water and hydrates in turn. The hydration, therefore, favours the activation of the germination process.

The synthesis of enzymes and hormones, provides an activation of the metabolic processes of the seed, characterized by:

An increase in enzymatic activity (in particular, enzymes that degrade sugars).

An increase in the breathing process

An increase in the degradation processes of the seed reserve substances (starch, lipids and proteins)

Inflow of soluble molecules to the embryonic tissues of the growing seed.

Also, from the point of view of the hormonal picture, there is a decrease in germination inhibitory hormones (ABA = abscisic acid) and a corresponding increase in germination promoting hormones (auxins, gibberellins and cytokinins).

The activation of the seed ends with the rootlet leaking from the seed, preceded by an intense growth phase of the embryo, during which the structure leaks from its envelope.

During Phase 2 of digestion and distribution of the seed substances, the reserve substances (starch, lipids, proteins, etc.), degraded to soluble and simpler substances (glucose, fatty acids and amino acids), are then transferred into the growth tissues.

Finally, once we reach Phase 3 where the structure of the seedling is now evident, it is possible to observe an axis where the cotyledons (i.e. the primordial leaves) are inserted.

On this axis it is possible to distinguish the radicle (the part that will develop downwards that will originate the roots) and the plumula (the part that will develop upwards that will originate the stem and leaves).

The germination of the seed in turn depends on intrinsic and extrinsic factors.

The intrinsic factors are related to the genetic characteristics of the species, such as:

- Species
- Variety
- Presence of hormones.

The extrinsic factors are instead related to environmental characteristics, such as:

- Water
- Temperature
- Oxygen
- Light
- Health status.

Germinability and viability of seeds

Knowledge of the process and the factors that regulate seed germination, is fundamental both for direct sowing in the open field and in the setting up of seedbeds in greenhouses, in order to understand what the optimal conditions are in order to obtain a prompt germination of the seeds and a uniform growth of the seedlings.

For this reason, the germination of a seed is influenced by its vitality and germinability.

The vitality of a seed is the characteristic of maintaining the physiological functions unchanged over time.

This property depends on the:

- Intrinsic characteristics (species and varieties)
- Extrinsic characteristics (e.g. growing environment, temperature and humidity of the species).

Depending on the vitality of the seeds, herbaceous species can be classified:

1. Short-lived (about 3 years e.g. chicory and lettuce)

2. Intermediate life (about 4 years e.g. barley, bean, rye, wheat and spelt)
3. Long life (about 5 years and more e.g. onion, chard, chickpea, watermelon, melon, pumpkin and zucchini, carrot, lettuce, tomato, eggplant and corn).

The germinability of a seed is the percentage probability that a viable seed will give rise to a new plant.

For this reason, from a commercial point of view, it is necessary that the seeds have minimum germinability values, which in turn vary according to specific characteristics.

Based on the percentage values of germinability, the species are divided into:

1. low germinability 65% (e.g. basil, carrot, endive, radicchio, parsley, pepper and aubergine)
2. Medium - low germinability 70% (e.g. asparagus, chard, cauliflower, broccoli, fennel, radish and celery)
3. Medium germinability 75% (e.g. watermelon, cabbage, Savoy cabbage, Brussels sprouts, melon, courgette, thistle, lettuce, common bean, tomato and spinach)
4. Highly germinal 80% (e.g. turnip, cucumber, pumpkin, Spanish bean, pea and broad bean).

The temperature is certainly the most important factor regulating seed germination, together with the optimal humidity conditions of the growing medium.

Depending on the optimal germination temperatures, horticultural species are divided into:

- At high temperature requirements 30 - 35 °C (pumpkin, courgette, watermelon, melon, etc.).
- At medium temperature requirements 20 - 30 °C (tomato, pepper, aubergine, etc.).
- At low temperature requirements 20 - 25 °C (lettuce, celery, spinach and asparagus).

The period required for seed germination is also linked to the thermal conditions of the growing medium.

About the moisture content of the substrate as a factor regulating the germinability of a seed, the species are divided into:

1. At low humidity level with conditions close to the withering point P.A. (e.g. pumpkin, melon, watermelon, pepper and radish)
2. At medium humidity level (e.g. cucumber, bean, pea, carrot, onion, spinach and tomato)
3. High humidity with conditions close to C.C. field capacity. (e.g. lettuce, chard and celery).

Horticultural species, unlike tree species, do not show phenomena of seed dormancy, at least the commercial ones regularly preserved and dried. In this case the lack of germination is due to the presence of old or badly preserved seeds.

An exception to this last characteristic are the species belonging to the Umbellifer or Apiaceae family (carrot, celery, fennel and parsley), where the reduced germinability of the seeds is due to the presence of embryos that are not very mature or absent despite the presence of reserve substances.

Seed quality

The quality of the seed is an important and fundamental requirement to be considered both in the case of direct sowing in the open field and to produce seedlings in nurseries for transplanting.

The quality of the seed is for this in turn dependent on:

1. Germinability of the seed
2. Seed purity
3. Calibration uniformity
4. Seed health
5. Genetic heritage of the variety.

Seed health can be easily verified in the laboratory with incubation tests in selective substrates that can detect the presence of phytopathogenic bacteria. In order to identify viruses, a visual and accurate control of freshly germinated seedlings is required.

The genetic characteristics of the variety can only be evaluated in the field and when the plants and seeds are harvested. This requires the use of certified seed with high germination guarantees and genetic resistance to diseases corresponding to those declared.

Plant Transplanting

Transplanting is the technique of planting seeds, which involves a phase of breeding the seedlings in greenhouses, before being transferred in open field.

Among the advantages of the technique we remember:

1. Advance of the production cycle
2. Earlier production (e.g. spring production) both in the open field and in greenhouses
3. Shorter growing cycle than a plant sown directly
4. Land use for several crops in the same year
5. Elimination of failures
6. Less competition with weeds
7. Greater uniformity of growth of seedlings
8. Better spacing of seedlings
9. Possibility of using transplanting machines (working capacity of 1 ha of about 6 - 12 hours)

One of the disadvantages will be:

- Higher costs for setting up the nursery and seedbeds.
- Rooting problems of seedlings
- Shallower root system
- Plants most subject to water stress
- Plants most prone to transplant stress

The very expensive transplanting technique, mainly used for F1 hybrid vegetables or plants available in small quantities, involves structuring a horticultural nursery with the production of plants precisely and without losses.

A modern horticultural nursery is organised as follows:

1. Receipt of order
2. Substrate control.
    a. Purchase.
    b. Chemical/physical analysis.

c. Phytotoxicity test.
   d. Preparation.
3. Seed control.
   a. Purchase.
   b. Germinability tests.
   c. treatments before germination.
4. Sowing programming.
5. Sowing in containers.
6. Germination in humid chambers or climatic cells.
   a. Staking.
   b. Repotting.
7. Transfer of seedlings to growth greenhouses.
   a. Acclimatisation.
   b. Irrigation.
   c. Fertilisation.
   d. Pesticide treatments.
   e. Use of phyto-regulators.
   f. Hardening.
8. Packing and shipping.
9. Recovery and sterilization of containers.

Production of plants intended for transplanting

The production of the seedlings in a horticultural nursery, to be destined to the following transplanting, can be done by resorting to:

- Bare-root seedlings
- Floor plans with earthen bread.

In a horticultural nursery, the production of seedlings with earthen bread can be carried out using the following systems, such as:

1. Sowing in paper jars
2. Sowing in honeycombed containers
3. Sowing in peat jars

Sowing in paper jars involves the use of hexagonal section jars (paper pots), glued together and placed on recoverable aluminium trays.

The paperpots:

1. They are produced in different sizes (from 3 to 10 cm)
2. They are used according to the needs of the crops
3. Large-scale processing lines suitable for automatic filling and/or sowing are used
4. In the most efficient solutions, the glue that holds the jars together can be peeled off with water in order to facilitate the spacing and planting of the seedlings.

Sowing in honeycombed containers consists in the use of polystyrene or polypropylene containers, from which the seedlings can be extracted with the substrate together with the roots.

This system provides:

1. Production of automated lines for filling and sowing
2. More advanced solutions with automatic sowing of about 400 boxes per hour
3. Filling of about 20 to 150 cavities using 2 people

Finally, sowing in peat jars involves the use of peat to pack containers in 80-litre bales that are humidified at the time of use.

This system allows:

1. Elimination of the problem of jars
2. The seedlings are separated from the cube at the time of planting.
3. Use of dicing machines able to produce cubes from 3 to 7 cm with an hourly capacity of 2000 - 12000 cubes.
4. Precision Sowing
5. Use both naked and candied seeds.

The main substrates used for sowing in nurseries are mixtures based on:

1. Blond peat
2. Brown peat
3. Perlite
4. Vermiculite.

The substrates before they are used, they must be:

1. Chemically controlled
2. Physiologically controlled (with plant growth tests)
3. Checked from a phytosanitary point of view for toxic residues of salts and/or pesticides and pests.

The stages following sowing in containers shall include

1. Transfer of the containers to humid chambers for a few days, with high humidity and temperature between 15 and 25 °C.
2. Constant wetting of containers and seedlings by automatic irrigation to shorten germination times and uniformity of births

3. Once the emergence of the seedlings has occurred, staking is carried out to standardise the subsequent growth
4. Transfer of seedlings into larger containers
5. Hardening stage. Hardening is the technique that aims to increase the resistance of young seedlings to physical, water, chemical, transport and transplanting stresses before they are marketed. The hardening technique is carried out by trying to stimulate cross resistance, according to which a seedling, when subjected to slight stress, becomes resistant to stress of a different nature. Hardening makes it possible to increase the dry matter content in the plant and consequently reduce its moisture content in order to increase resistance to cold, especially for early spring sowing vegetable varieties.

The hardening of seedlings can be achieved by using various systems such as:

1. Use of reduced water regimes (during the last 10 days of nursery stay)
2. Use of differentiated temperatures (with modification of the morphological and physiological characteristics of the seedling)
3. Controlling plant nutrition through balanced regimes
4. Use of chemical substances (CCC cycocel or PP-333 pacobutrazole), capable of modifying the growth of the seedlings.

CHAPTER 10 - How to Control Atmospheric Temperature and Humidity

The two main elements to be managed in an unheated greenhouse and tunnel are atmospheric humidity and temperature, elements that affect crops. As a general rule, the optimum atmospheric humidity to be recorded during the winter in these protections must be 60-70 %, while the minimum temperature must be around 2-3 °C, values which occur using a hygrometer and a thermometer recording the maximum and minimum temperatures respectively.

Atmospheric Humidity

The atmospheric humidity, which is spontaneously created in a greenhouse and in an unheated tunnel, must always be kept under control, especially during the coldest periods, when the formation of water drops on the inner wall of the roofing sheets of the structures is not uncommon, water falling on the crops causes widespread and dangerous rotting.

If high, that is close to 80-90%, the atmospheric humidity settles also on the vegetables keeping them wet for long time, causing rottenness of fungal origin. For this reason, it is necessary to favour the exchange of air in the protections to eliminate the excess atmospheric humidity by intervening on the openings.

In autumn, spring and summer it is not difficult to regulate the atmospheric humidity inside the protections. The operation is more complicated during the winter, when it is also necessary to maintain the minimum growth temperature of the vegetables (which generally ranges from 3 to 5°C).

During the coldest periods, it is necessary to avoid airing the protections in the early morning hours, as the extremely rigid external temperature would lower the internal one, taking advantage, on the contrary, of the "less cold" temperatures of the central hours of the day, providing for the closing of the openings before sunset, in such a way that the last sun of the day favours the increase of the internal temperature, useful to counteract the night thermal decrease.

Opening the protections during the winter for a few hours a day (i.e. in the order of 2-3) is enough to keep the excess atmospheric humidity under control. This operation does not necessarily have to be carried out every day, as only two openings per week may be enough.

However, it is necessary to avoid opening the protections on very cold days and in the presence of rain or fog, as the external atmospheric humidity may be higher than the internal one. After the winter, the protections are gradually ventilated (usually from March) until they are left completely open all day, perhaps closing them in the late afternoon if the nights are still cool, and then reopening them in the late morning. At the end of spring and during the summer the protections should always be left open, even at night.

Temperature

Another important element that affects the outcome of harvests during the winter is the temperature, which in the early hours of a cold morning with -5°C outside (when the thermal inversion causes both outside and inside temperatures to drop sharply) in an unheated greenhouse or tunnel can be as low as -3°C or at most 1 degree below zero.

In this type of protection, not having devices which heat the atmosphere, in order to defend the vegetables from the low temperatures it is necessary to use a veil of non-woven fabric (weighing at least 15-17 grams per square metre), to be spread directly on the cultivations, to be removed at the moment of the harvest and to be repositioned immediately afterwards; in case of very cold days, it is advisable to prepare two veils on the plants.

Always in order to protect the vegetables from the frost, if you live in particularly cold areas of the Centre-North, we suggest you to install inside the protections, especially in the tunnels, a second cover, formed by a smaller tunnel which has the function to further protect the cultivations from the cold and to limit the dripping on them. The drops of water, which form mainly on the inner side of the main cover, fall on the cover of the smaller tunnel and therefore not on the vegetables below. The crops can be protected from frost by installing small tunnels directly on the growing beds, with cover sheets made of transparent plastic film 0,07-0,1 micron thick. In this way the vegetables are grown under a double tunnel, inside which the temperature will be ideal especially for the cultivation of leafy vegetables such as lettuce and chicory, vegetables that could not give good harvests if grown in a normal unheated tunnel.

Watering

In order to ensure ideal growing conditions for vegetables grown under this type of protection, irrigation must also be taken care of, bearing in mind that it is always done indoors, with very different characteristics compared to open field conditions. After a rain, a cultivation in open field should not be irrigated, while under a greenhouse or a tunnel thing are different, because the protective cover does not allow the rain to reach the crops. For this reason, plants must always be guaranteed a moderately moist soil.

In addition, an unheated greenhouse or tunnel are often closed environments, where evapotranspiration is much lower than in the open field. For this reason, the frequency of irrigation and the amount of water supplied must also be reduced. Good rule, therefore, is to control the humidity of the soil before irrigating, operating according to the needs of the plants. The best hours to irrigate an unheated protection are in the morning, using water at room temperature (i.e. left to rest in bins for at least one day) so as not to cause thermal stress to the roots of the vegetables and provide the plants with a water reserve to draw on during the day.

Kevin S. Stevenson
Greenhouse Gardening For Beginners

CHAPTER 11 - Pests and Diseases

Plant pests and diseases can affect even the most well-groomed flowers and vegetables and affect even the most experienced gardeners. Knowing how to recognise them is important and not complicated, not even for beginners.

Vegetable Diseases and Pests

All living organisms are subject to disease, both in the animal and plant kingdoms; diseases, of any kind and origin, stress the organism and can be the cause or trigger of other pathologies, in a chain of events that sometimes has some incredible.

Healthy and robust plants resist to the attack of diseases and parasites much better than weak or stressed ones, but this resistance is not an absolute guarantee; in fact, in spite of a correct cultivation, a careful weeding, the rotation of the crops and the selection of an increasing quantity of varieties resistant to diseases, even in the vegetable gardens cultivated with extreme care, problems of parasites and diseases can occur. Knowing how to diagnose the various diseases quickly and accurately is essential to be able to intervene as soon as possible with the right care, which very often involves the administration of chemical substances. Horticultural varieties are particularly delicate because unlike ornamental species they are very often destined for food consumption, with obvious health and ethical considerations.

Precautions when using agrochemicals

Always follow the manufacturer's instructions precisely, as regards dilution, application time and the period between the last application and the time of harvesting.

Keep these products tightly closed and labelled so that they are not accessible to children or animals. Never transfer them into beverage bottles. Spray on non-windy days so that the product does not fall on other plants or in nearby gardens, ponds, streams, springs or ditches. Never use for mixing or spraying containers already used for herbicides and never prepare more solution than is necessary, because then it is difficult to eliminate the excess without danger. Wash your hands and used instruments thoroughly after application.

These standards are almost always also present in the product leaflets.

Due to their nature, some chemicals must be used with even greater precautions. For example, calomel powder is poisonous and protective gloves must be worn while handling. Many substances can irritate the skin, eyes, nose and mouth; allergy sufferers should wear gloves, mask and goggles; some studies would also seem to indicate a carcinogenic risk of several substances, but at the moment there are no definite and incontrovertible data.

Using pesticides must always be done with extreme caution: not all insects and animals in the garden are harmful to plants, indeed there are some useful ones, think of pollinating insects (bees and the like), fundamental for the development of many fruits. They can be killed by pesticides, which is why they should not be used in excess and indiscriminately.

Pesticides and Fungicides

Fungicides are used to prevent infections while pesticides are used to combat infestations. There are many types of pesticides and they act in different ways. Those that act by contact (e.g. derris), directly affect insects: to kill the maximum amount of them, it is important to distribute these substances over the entire surface of the plant. After application they remain active for a relatively short period of time. Substances that act by translocation are absorbed by the plant and spread through the sap; they are very effective against lymph sucking insects. It is not necessary to spray the whole plant, but only the roots can be wetted. Most fungicides only prevent disease and should therefore be applied before the symptoms of an infection occur. Fungicides that act partially by translocation can now be found on the market. These products are partly absorbed by the tissues of the plant and act for a short period even if the infection is already in progress.

Methods of application

Chemicals can be purchased in the form of powders, soluble powders, sprays, ointments, pills, granules, aerosols. However, not all of them exist under each of these forms, nor are all forms effective for a certain type of disease or infestation. Most of these products are indicated in the text according to the active chemicals they contain and not according to name or brand. Always check that the most suitable active ingredients are contained; these are written on package labels or package leaflets.

Plant Diseases

Parsnip Cancer

It causes parsnip tissue rot. There are no effective remedies, but you can reduce the risk of an attack by growing the plants in a cool place, renewed every year, in a well tilled soil with a pH of 5.5-7.0.

Cabbage hernia (Plasmodiophora brassicae)

It deforms the roots and seriously compromises the development of all brassicas. This disease is more frequent in acidic soils; the pH of the soil can therefore be increased to 6,5-7,5 by distributing calcium cyanamide or calcium carbonate at a rate of 450 g/m2; maintain the degree of acidity at this level with small additions of the same substances in the following years. The 4% calomel dust incorporated into the soil at a rate of 45 g/m2 before sowing helps to combat hernia and is also effective against cabbage root fly. Seedlings can also be soaked in calomel powder or a benomyl solution as a preventive measure.

Alonate or charcoal spotting (Pseudomonas phaseolicola)

It is a bacterial infection that affects the seeds causing stains on the bean leaves. The stains are surrounded by a slightly coloured halo. There are no known effective remedies; diseased plants should be burned after harvesting.

Leaf spotting

It mainly affects brassicas, beets and beets by attacking the older leaves on which round, brown spots remain. Sometimes the affected tissues fall, and holes remain. It is a disease that worsens in the wetter seasons, especially in crowded crops or on brassicas that have grown too tender due to an excess of nitrogen fertilizers. The infected leaves must be removed and destroyed. How to prevent thinning plants and carry out careful crop rotation.

Bad asparagus wine (Rhizoctonia violacea)

It attacks the roots and the base of the asparagus growing wrapped around them in purplish filaments. Small round masses of fungal hyphae may also appear. With the death of the roots the vegetative apexes yellow and die. If the infection is light, the contaminated area can be isolated by introducing thick polyethylene sheets into the soil at a depth of 30 cm. If it is serious, leave the infected soil and transfer the cultivation elsewhere. Seedling collar rot is favoured by conditions of stagnant or overcrowded air and the common use of unsterilized garden compound. The affected seedlings rot at collar height and collapse to the ground. As a prevention sowing in sterilized compost. Light infections can be kept under control by watering seedlings with captan, zineb or Chesthunt compost, after removing already dead seedlings, to avoid the risk of infection.

Onion rot (Botrytis allii)

It can destroy a large amount of onions stored for storage. A grey mould grows on or near the collar of the bulbs, making them soft and rotting. Then the large black spores of the fungus develop on the rotting tissues. Store only firm, dry bulbs in a cool, dry place with good ventilation all around. Check them often and discard those that begin to rot immediately. Since the infection can start from the seed, only buy good quality seedlings or seedlings already treated against rotting in a reputable shop. Sprinkle seeds and seedlings with benomyl powder before sowing or transplanting.

Black potato rot (Erwinia carotovora var. atroseptica)

It causes the early yellowing of the affected plants' foliage; the shoots fall due to rotting and blackening at the base, even if sometimes some stems can develop normally. The plant can die before tubers form, and those already formed have a slimy brown or grey rottenness inside them. Destroy any infected plant. If severely affected tubers are kept, they will rot, while those only slightly affected with no symptoms can go unnoticed but, if planted the following season, will transmit the infection.

Pedal and root rot

They are caused by different species of fungi that affect the roots and the stem base of young plants and kill them. As a prevention soak the seedlings in captan; at first symptoms water the plants immediately with a solution of captan, Chesthunt compound or zineb. For affected tomato plants tamp down sterile compost around the base. Burn diseased plants.

Moniliosis (Sclerotinia)

It affects the roots and the base of the stems of various plants, including carrots, cucumbers, Jerusalem artichokes, and the roots and tubers stored for storage. Burn the affected plants to prevent the infection from spreading to the rest of the soil through the large spores that form on diseased plants. Unfortunately, there are no suitable chemicals. Cleaning and rotation of affected crops are the only practical remedies that can be taken.

White onion mould (Sclerotium cepivorum)

It appears as a white felt at the base of the onions; it quickly causes the death of the leaves. Burn the plants as soon as you realize they are sick. As a prevention distribute 4% benomyl or calomel dust directly into the furrows before sowing or by spraying the plants with a benomyl solution when they have reached a height of 18-20 cm.

Grey mould (Botrytis cinerea)

It can affect most plants at any stage of development. It is favoured by overcrowding conditions and stagnant air; the stems, leaves or fruits affected rot quickly and are covered by a grey-brown mould. As a prevention sow well-spaced and thin out seedlings and plants. Ventilate greenhouse crops well and ensure that dead or rotting plant material is removed and burned. Spray wintering plants with thiram. If grey mould affects all greenhouse plants, fumigate with tecnazene.

Grey mould of legumes (Botrytis cinerea)

It causes discoloration of the leaves and stems of the broad beans and can attack wintering crops with serious consequences. Plants grown in acidic soils or those that grow too soft due to excess nitrogen fertilizers are most affected. As a prevention, sow rarely, distribute potash at a rate of 15 g/m2 before sowing in November and keep the pH of the soil between 6.5 and 7.0. In areas where grey mould is endemic, spray the still young foliage with a cupric fungicide before the symptoms of grey mould occur.

Hate or bad white

It attacks zucchini, cucumbers and other vegetables, especially when the roots do not have enough water. A white powder covers the stems and leaves. At first symptoms spray the affected plants with benomyl and, if necessary, repeat the treatment.

Peronospora

It can attack lettuce, onions, spinach and young brassicas. Sow well-spaced and thin out the seedlings in good time; if they are equally attached, remove all diseased leaves and spray with zineb or mancozeb. For the young cauliflower plants, you can also use dichlofluanid and on the other brassicas, onions and spinach the Bordeaux mush; for the lettuce is also good for the thiram.

Solanaceae downy mildew (Phytophthora infestans)

And a serious potato disease that also affects tomatoes. The leaves, stems and tubers of potatoes can be destroyed. To reduce the risk of infection, plant healthy tubers in holes at least 12 cm deep and tamp them down at the right time. Potatoes grown for the autumn harvest should also be sprayed with mancozeb, zineb or Bordeaux mush from July onwards. Cut and remove the stems before harvesting the tubers. In areas where this disease is widespread, plant varieties of potatoes that are resistant to downy mildew. Protect the tomatoes by spraying them in mid-summer immediately after topping with one of the products suitable for potatoes. If the weather is cool and humid, repeat the treatment every two or three weeks.

Common mange

It occurs mainly when the soil is arid, lacking in humus and in alkaline soils. A pH of 5.0-6.0 in the soil and an enrichment of the humus content reduce the incidence of this disease. In addition, the potatoes should be kept well irrigated, especially when the weather is dry. There are no effective chemicals against scabies.

Virosis

They cause leaf spots, deformations and often a stunted development of the plants. They attack mainly courgettes, celery, cucumbers and tomatoes, but also other vegetables. They are spread by aphids and nematodes; it is therefore necessary to keep these parasites under control and destroy the weeds, which serve as a receptacle. For infected plants there is no remedy: once the evil has been diagnosed the only thing to do is to burn them. Always wash your hands and tools very well after coming into contact with plants affected by virosis.

Vermin

Aphids

They infest most crops. In addition to the damage that aphids directly cause, they are carriers of virosis and promote the development of soot. Keep the plants under regular control; in case of attack nebulize with dimethoate, derris, formothion, malathion, menazon, pyrimidil or similar products. If harvesting should take place no more than one week after treatment, spray with derris. It is advisable to spray also the pumpkins only with derris or pyrethroids, otherwise they could be damaged; on the contrary, the peas and beans, if in flower, must be sprayed at dusk with pyrimidil, tolerated by the bees which are the main pollinators.

Root aphids (Pemphigus bursarius)

They can hit beans, lettuce and artichokes. Usually you do not notice the attack until the plants are infested. In case of serious infestation spray with malathion. As a prevention, distribute diazinon granules on the soil before sowing or transplanting.

Aleurodide or Greenhouse Whitefly (Trialeurodes vaporariorum)

It attacks brassicas, pumpkins, tomatoes and other vegetables and leaves soot deposits on the leaves. The cabbage whitefly is a species distinct from the greenhouse whitefly, but pyrethroid or pyrimiphos-methyl treatments are effective against both, spraying three or four times at seven-day intervals. In greenhouses, it is possible to resort to the integrated pest control by introducing the wasp Encarsia, thus avoiding the problem of the residues left by the pesticides and the habituation, but for most gardeners, unluckily, this method is not very practical.

Pole or land fleas (Phy/lotreta spp)

They are tiny beetles that infest the brassica seedlings in large numbers, devouring the leaves on which they leave small holes. Use derris, HCH or pirimiphos-methyl treatments. Plants are rarely damaged after they have passed the seedling stage.

Caterpillars

They attack cabbages and you must prevent them from penetrating to the heart, because it would be very difficult to reach them here. They can be removed by hand, if the number of plants is limited, or they can be treated with carbaryl, HCH or fenitrothion.

Snails, onyxes and centipedes

They can destroy seedlings and attack many developing vegetables. Against snails distribute along the rows of lures of metaldehyde or methiocarb. The latter is more effective against onisks and centipedes, but if the infestation is severe, it may be necessary to sprinkle seedlings with HCH powder.

Asparagus cryoceris (Crioceris asparagus)

It is a small yellow and black insect whose grey-black larvae can defoliate plants during the summer. Suppress them by spraying the asparagus with derris or pirimiphos-methyl as soon as you notice their presence.

Dorifora (Leptinotarsa decemlineata)

It is a parasite that affects the Solanaceae, especially potatoes and aubergines and, to a lesser extent, peppers and tomatoes. It attacks first the shoots and young leaves, then the other parts of the plants until they are completely defoliated. Afterwards, the plants can die. Soak affected plants with carbaryl.

Elaterides (Agriotes spp)

They can be found in large numbers in meadows and weed-infested areas. They attack the roots of many vegetables can seriously affect the quality of potatoes. Treat the soil when planting or sowing with diazinon or bromophos.

Celery fly (Phillophylla heraclei)

It lives in the leaves of celery, parsnip and some aromatic herbs. Against the most serious attacks nebulize the plants with malathion or dimethoate. If the infestation is light, however, remove the flies by hand and burn the affected leaves.

Carrot fly (Psila rosae)

It is the most harmful parasite of the carrot and attacks parsley, parsnip and celery. Plant growth is stunted, and secondary rot can develop in carrots already affected. Sow very seldom or use casing seeds by carefully arranging them so that you no longer need to thin out the plants afterwards, because the female of this pest is strongly attracted to the scent that is released from the carrot leaves during thinning. By sowing after the end of May you can avoid the first generation of larvae, but carrot flies are so common that it is advisable to sprinkle the sowing furrows with diazinon, bromophos or chlorpyrifos, in order to protect them for at least six to eight weeks. Nebulize with pirimiphos-methyl at the end of August carrots that are not harvested before autumn.

Onion fly (Chlortophila antiqua)

It attacks all plants belonging to the onion family. Young plants can be destroyed by the larvae and already developed bulbs are excavated by tunnels that make them inedible. During the early, more vulnerable stages of development, disinfect the soil with diazinon, bromophos or chlorpyrifos granules when sowing or transplanting.

Cabbage root fly (Chlortophila brassicae)

At the larva stage it can devastate the seedlings and young plants of many brassicas. Seeding furrows and planting soil should be treated in advance with diazinon, chlorpyrifos or bromophos. Against attacks on already well-established plants water abundantly with pirimiphos-methyl.

Onion Nematode (Ditylenchus dipsaci)

It attacks mainly plants belonging to the onion family, but also carrots, parsnips and beans. Nematodes are microscopic worm-like creatures that live inside the stems and leaves. Because of them the plant tissues become swollen and mushy and the plant does not take long to rot and die. For an amateur gardener there are no substances capable of suppressing this parasite and infested plants must be burned. Plants that can be attacked by nematodes, including some weeds, should not be grown in onion nematode infested soil for several years.

Golden potato nematode (Heterodera rostochiensis)

It lives in the roots of the potatoes and tomatoes and already by mid-summer the foliage is totally dead; the harvest is therefore very small. There are no chemicals available for amateur gardeners; crop rotation helps as a prevention, but if a soil is seriously infested, it may be necessary to stop growing potatoes. Some varieties of potatoes are resistant to a nematode species, Globodera rostochiensis, but none are so far resistant to G. pallida.

Nottue

They are caterpillars of different species of lepidoptera living in the ground. They feed on the roots and base of the stems of plants and attack most vegetables when they are still at an early stage, first withering and then dying. As a treatment, disinfect the soil with chlorpyrifos, dazino or bromophos before sowing or transplanting.

Red greenhouse spider (Tetranychus telarius)

It is a very common pest of vegetables grown in greenhouses and causes discoloration of the leaves and a halt in development. It has tiny dimensions: it is almost invisible to the naked eye. A humid atmosphere helps to keep away the red spiders, which thrive in hot and dry conditions, but to cope with the infestations spray the plants at seven-day intervals with malathion, dimethoate or pirimiphos-methyl. When using these substances on cucumbers be careful because they can damage the leaves; a less risky alternative is integrated pest control. Spray in the evening when it is less hot and make sure the roots of the plants are well moist.

Sitona leguminous plants (Sitona lineatus and S. limosus)

It feeds on the edge of the leaves of pea and bean plants. It is only necessary to use HCH or pirimiphos-methyl powder if seedlings are attached.

Pea turret (Cydia nigricana)

At the larva stage it seriously damages the peas, eating the fruit and compromising cultivation, especially in the case of late ripening varieties. Earlier varieties are generally not attacked because they flower before laying their eggs. Spray the peas that bloom between mid-June and mid-August, seven to ten days after flowering, with fenitrothion.

Pea tripe (Kakothrips pisivorus)

It is a very small and thin insect, brown-black or yellow, which sucks the sap from the leaves and pods of peas. This causes a silver-brown discoloration and the damaged pods can grow deformed and have only a few fruits. The most serious infestations occur especially in summer, when it is hot and dry. As a prevention nebulize with dimethoate, formothion or fenitrothion.

Birds

They can cause damage to crop throughout the year. Scarecrows and repellents are rarely effective; in some cases and only for short periods they can help, but if the problem of birds is constantly recurring, it is essential to use some kind of cage and protective net for plants and fruits so that the crops are not compromised.

CONCLUSION

Thank you for making it through to the end of this book, let's hope it was informative and able to provide you with all the tools you need to achieve your goals whatever they may be.

Greenhouse gardening has emerged as a great way to grow organic and genuine products to gain good health. Yet, not everyone gets the benefits of this wonderful process due to lack of knowledge of the process. This book has tried to bring all the important points on the forefront so that you can get all the benefits of greenhouse gardening without having to face the negative effects.

All you need to do is follow the information given in the book and stick to the adopted routine.

You can also get all the benefits of the process by following the simple steps given in the book.

I hope that this book can help you in achieving your goals.

Kevin S. Stevenson
Greenhouse Gardening For Beginners

www.ingramcontent.com/pod-product-compliance
Lightning Source LLC
Chambersburg PA
CBHW050300120526
44590CB00016B/2429